RAINFORESTS
FOR BEGINNERS

NAOMI ROSENBLATT

D0775808

Writers and Readers

WRITERS AND READERS PUBLISHING, INCORPORATED
P.O. Box 461, Village Station
New York, NY 10014

A Writers and Readers Documentary Comic Book
Copyright © 1992
ISBN # 0-86316-005-0
1 2 3 4 5 6 7 8 9 0

Manufactured in the United States of America

recycled paper

In memory of Albert M. Fiering
(1923 - 1990)

Keep stretching a bow
You repent of the pull,
A whetted saw
Goes thin and dull,
Surrounded with treasure
You lie ill at ease,
Proud beyond measure
You come to your knees:
Do enough without vieing.
Be living, not dying.
-- Lao Tzu, The Way of Life

Thanks and Acknowledgments

Many people's input and support made *Rainforests for Beginners* possible.

Glenn Thompson, the man behind the *for Beginners* books, deserves credit for his expansive thinking at a restricted time for book publishing.

Karen Sideman made the invaluable contribution of a computer and laser printer. She was not only reliable and generous; she was interested enough in my work to volunteer excellent editorial feedback and help create the cover.

Specialists and writers in the "rainforest community" were exceptionally forthcoming with their resources and time. I thank the following among them for interviewing with me and offering feedback as the book took form:

Dr. Michael J. Balick, Director, Institute of Economic Botany of the New York Botanical Gardens, **Dr. Jason Clay**, Research Director of Cultural Survival, **Helouisa B. Edwards**, Advisor, Fundacao Biodiversitas, author **Eric Hansen**, **Daniel R. Katz**, President of the Rainforest Alliance of New York, author **Joe Kane**, **Dr. Christine Padoch**, Associate Scientist at the New York Botanical Gardens, **Marjorie Scott** of the Rainforest Action Network.

Friends and family outdid themselves clipping articles, copy editing and proofing my manuscript, and simply keeping me in good spirits. Those in the Bay Area provided unforgettable hospitality. **Lawrence E. Joseph**, author of *Gaia: The growth of an Idea*, lent a fine editorial eye to rid this book of its many parasitic spelling and grammatical errors. **Shey Wolvek-Pfister** and **Sam Moore** helped design the cover, and took over last-minute typesetting. **Bill Stewart** and **Kevin Silva** at the Superior Copy Center, 228 East 10th St., really did a superior job making stats. Other friends deserve mention for their contribution (however etheric) and comraderie during producton:

Aradia, Mitch Berger, Jonathan Blunk, Angela Bocage, Gary Brenner, Sue Burish, Martha Carroll, Darcy Di Mona, Holly Ewald, Anne Finkelstein, Eike Gebhardt, Dave Gilden, Magdalena Gomez, Kenyon Gordon, Sarah Haviland, Don and Diane Holmes, Jim Miller, Nanna Nilson, James O'Malley, James Pritchard, the Rabens family, Lelia Ruckenstein, Roz Saltzman, Sheila Samton, Carl Schnedeker, Jennie Schacht, Deborah Weiss and James Whitman.

Last, and most, I thank my family. **Aaron and Judy Rosenblatt**, my folks, offered tremendous assistance and hospitality, meticulously proofreading as only parents can. My uncle, Gestalt therapist and writer **Daniel Rosenblatt** inspired me with his example of courage and sharp wit. My sister **Leah Rosenblatt** encouraged me with her own brilliant lyrics and original music. And, speaking of song, I can still hear the voice of my deceased aunt, **Diana Rosenblatt**, singing:

> just like a tree standing by the water, we shall not be moved..."

Table of Contents

Ntroduction

Ladies and gentlemen--

I know a sure thing when I see one! Can't complain, I've raked in billions, I've helped the Third World pay off its foreign debt and I've provided employment for starving peasants.

Cattle ranches, dams, export crops, gold mines, oil wells, power plants, timber concessions... tropical rainforests rain opportunity!

It's the last frontier, folks.

This is the only overgrown, idle land where Nature still paralyzes development. But within the next fifty years, we will productively transform ALL of it!

I'm getting in on the action... Onward Ho!

The forest protects your land, water and climate. She offers fruit, nuts, spices, gums, medicines, a home to many people and to half of all living species. Kill the forest and you kill yourself, forever...

What right have you to eliminate, in seconds, that which has grown over thousands, even millions, of years?

HELP!!!

Can't you see? Floods and mud slips in the Philippines, cyclones and monsoons in Bangladesh, and drought in California are all by-products of deforestation!

Do you realize that your decisions about who lives and who dies are irreversible?

What right have you to destroy my home, my food, my family?

HELP!!!

Thousands of plants with medicinal compounds grow in rainforests. Cures for cancer, heart disease and viruses have been found already. But only 1% of these plants has been studied! Wish they'd hurry up and find cures to stupidity, arrogance, greed and deceit!

7

IMAGINE Earth "at the dawn of history... covered with immense primeval forests, in which scattered clearings must have appeared like islets in an ocean of green." [1]

Trees lived on this planet for hundreds of millions of years before we did.

Remains of the most ancient trees compose oil and **coal**— literally, the **fossil fuels** upon which our economy pivots.

Photosynthesizing plants evolved maybe 430 million years ago. Small and close to the Earth's surface for their first hundred million years, their competitive quest for sunlight stretched them skyward. **And the ancestors of modern trees grew into lush, varied forests, which sheltered nearly two thirds of dry land masses for 300 million years.**

Some four million years ago, humanity's immediate forerunners appeared on the scene.

It is said that life in tropical treetops nurtured us into our present form: our ancestors' hands developed to grasp branches. Swinging through trees, their eyes learned to gauge distances. Trees also provided them with food and shelter.

No wonder the forests were our first cathedrals!

About 10,000 years ago people around the globe became farmers and settlers. Some civilizations relied more on farming than others.

But centuries of agricultural practice did not radically interfere with the forests' ancient ecosystem.

Only within the last 500 years -- with the advent of European colonizers -- has the tropical forest been converted to a hotbed of cash crops!

The New World's bounty spurred colonization. Europe had undergone its own "epoch of deforestation" and timber was scarce. Loggers and developers of fruit and sugar-cane plantations set a precedent of foreign exploitation. Later, North America was deforested in the 18th and 19th centuries by its new population. Now, at an accelerated 20th-century-rate, an "epoch of deforestation" has consumed the tropics. Since 1945, half the world's tropical rainforests have been mined, burned, bulldozed. The time has come to ask what the 21st century is likely to bring -- and what we can do to shape the rainforests' future.

Chapter 1: What and Where Are Rainforests?

"*Pieces of gold sown on the agate, mahogany pillars supporting an emerald dome bouquets of white satin and delicate stalks of rubies surround the water roses.*"

... A. Rimbaud
ILLUMINATIONS

From scrub jungle

....to savanna...

...to cloud forest

...tropical forests vary greatly.
Are all tropical forests rainforests?

O mind classifications!
Each of these rich,
wild expressions
of vegetation is so unique,
so abundant
in species variety that
no two acres
could sooner replace
each other than
could the content of any
two poems
or dreams!

True, but
tell-tale signs
distinguish

lowland, evergreen tropical rainforests.
They are the most lush, warm, wet and
biologically active of the many tropical
forest systems.

11

Table of Yearly Rainfall

approximately 150-400 inches
lowland evergreen rainforest

approximately 85-150 inches
seasonal or monsoon forest

approxiamtely 40-85 inches
"moist" or broad-leafed deciduous forest

when it rains it pours.

Lowland, evergreen rainforests receive more than 100 inches of rain each year, and have no dry or cool seasons. They grow near the Equator at low altitudes. Most of them are located in **Latin America**, in the Amazon River Basin, or along the coasts. **Southeast Asia** is the world's second-richest source of these rainforests.

That is what's meant by the buzzword **rainforest**. But rainforests grow anywhere the climate permits: **Africa, Australia, Hawaii, the South Sea and Caribbean islands.** Temperate rainforests grow in the **U.S. Pacific Northwest.**

When ocean winds move inland, they intercept columns of moisture that hover above tropical forests. Hence, clouds gather and rains fall, temperatures cool and ...

...gorillas may be seen in the mist!

I love to walk in the rain!

So do multitudes of birds, animals, plants and micro-organisms. Water is the basis of all life. Consistent light and warmth in the tropics also promote growth. What more "life-friendly" environment exists on land? **Lowland evergreen rainforests are the most diverse ecosystems.**

As well as the OLDEST ecosystems!

A thimble-full of rainforest soil may contain as many bacteria as there are people on Earth!

The wetter the better!

We decomposers thrive!

Water keeps us alive!

13

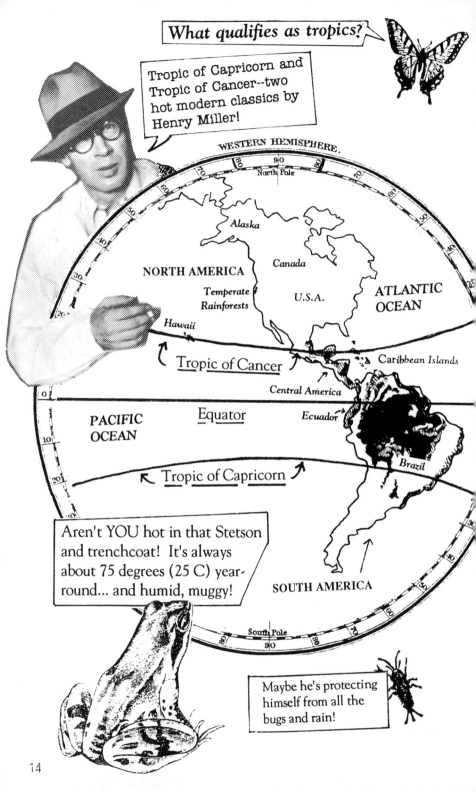

What qualifies as tropics?

Tropic of Capricorn and Tropic of Cancer--two hot modern classics by Henry Miller!

WESTERN HEMISPHERE.

North Pole

NORTH AMERICA

Alaska

Canada

U.S.A.

ATLANTIC OCEAN

Temperate Rainforests

Hawaii

Tropic of Cancer

Caribbean Islands

Central America

Equator

PACIFIC OCEAN

Ecuador

Brazil

Tropic of Capricorn

Aren't YOU hot in that Stetson and trenchcoat! It's always about 75 degrees (25 C) year-round... and humid, muggy!

SOUTH AMERICA

South Pole

Maybe he's protecting himself from all the bugs and rain!

The Tropic of Cancer and the Tropic of Capricorn are two parallels of latitude which fall 23.5 degrees respectively north and south of the equator. But as forest ecology expert Norman Myers advises, the tropics may be more accurately defined by their year-round warm temperatures than by lines on a map.

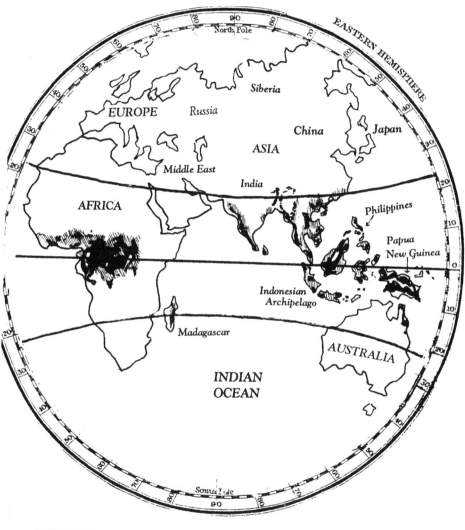

 Approximate Rainforest, before 1945
(Evergreen and Seasonal)
Approximate Remaining Rainforest

HOW IS A RAINFOREST LIKE
A LARGE, MODERN METROPOLIS?

A rainforest may be compared to a big city.
Both environments are jam-packed with
activity. Decadence gives rise to vitality.
Varieties of life forms compete, kill and
feed off each other, yet depend upon each
other for sustenance.

You city folk think you're
so **wild, original** and
flamboyant-- you ain't
seen nothing!

*Lotsa monkeying around
in the upper echelons!*

Epiphytes are kind of
vagabond vines. They have
no roots, and attach themselves
to tree trunks. Water, oxygen,
dust and decomposing
refuse sustain them.

What a housing crunch!
30 plants may grow
on a given trunk!

Try 50 species
of orchid alone!

12 insect and mite
species may live on a
single sloth!

When we say bio-diversity
we mean business!

There are predators and prey,
hosts and parasites, all competing
to survive and get to the top.

Like many cities, a rainforest is hierarchic. Those closer to the top monopolize resources. (In a rainforest, this resource is sunlight.) Adaptations are made by those further down. However, since most birds, mammals and even reptiles live in the canopy, the majority of rainforest residents have access to the critical resource. Therefore, distribution of "goods" is more fair and sensible in a rainforest than it tends to be in a modern city.

Another difference-- a rainforest is <u>clean</u>!

There are always big shots!

<u>EMERGENT TREES</u> are often the oldest trees, and have grown taller than those in the CANOPY layer.

The <u>CANOPY</u> is composed of interlocking tree crowns. It accommodates 2/3 of all species who live in the forest, and is said to be the most life-sustaining habitat on Earth.

The <u>UNDERSTORY</u> includes shrubs, vines, bushes, and young, small trees. This dark, wet layer may grow into a jungle.

There are "old boy networks." Trees reproduce with the help of birds, bats and insects. Meanwhile, decomposers and parasites take care of recycling soil nutrients.

Even New Yorker magazine wrote that in our millions of vest-pocket nooks and crannies, **millions of life forms quietly tick away...** 2

At the <u>FOREST FLOOR</u> seedlings and small animals receive some 1% of sunlight. It is cool, dark and moist. But soil is poor, because the minerals are locked in the plant layers.

The surface of the moon has been more thoroughly studied than the heart of the rainforest canopy.

Here's a parrot-dox: What is the sound of one wing flapping? Why are rainforests accessible to industry, but not to science?

The answer, my friend, is buzzin' in the chainsaws...

Simple answer! The lowland forests present no hills or rocky terrain. We can get in easily with our bulldozers, logging trucks and saws. Now, those cloud forests on mountains, THEY will be a challenge!

Complicated answer! We tropical biologists are underfunded and underequipped. We still use pencils, pads, canvas sacks and field glasses! How can we keep pace with those trucks?

In recent years this has started to change. If we find a medicinal plant whose financial yield could compete with that of cattle or timber, there may be hope.

Now, just a second! That's a lot of carbon dioxide!
I'll show you biomass! It's Census time:
okay, neighbors, enumerate yourselves!

20

Any forest "Census" must include us!
We are descendants of original
human rainforest dwellers. Our tribes
have lived here for centuries! We are the
Pygmies of the Ituri forest in Zaire,
the **Yanomami** of northern Brazil,
the **Huaorani** of Ecuador, the **Kayapo**
of southern Brazil's Xingu River basin,
the **Kuna** of Panama, the **Karen** of Burma,
the **Yali** of Indonesia, the **Maya** of Central
America, the **Penan** of Malaysia, to name but
nine of maybe two thousand tribes.

Like native tribes
of North America,
our land, food,
health, our cultures--
our very lives --
have become
endangered.

We tend to be hunters, gatherers and fishers. Often we live nomadically. We build camps in small clearings, from wood, vines and leaves.

Marked differences between industrialized, "1st World" values, and those of smaller tribal nations struck Eric Hansen when, in 1982, he visited the Malaysian state of Sarawak and met up with Borneo's Penan people.

He does not know how to hunt!

What is a man who doesn't hunt, and a woman who does not bear children?

Mr. Eric, why do people down-river commit violent acts?

Sure, we can understand stealing, in an emergency... but what is this rape and murder?

And what are supermarkets?

And most strange of all, what is suicide?

We Penan have never done this...

What would be a serious crime in the Penan community?

Being stingy, not sharing with others. This can cause bad feelings.

Funny-- in America, there are no laws against stinginess! Hoarding for oneself is esteemed and rewarded.

For us, a crime is an act which creates bad feeling among people...

Considering how close together you live, it is not surprising that the feelings of others are of the greatest importance.

...like adultery. The offenders must pay a fine!!

If you deceive your mate, it will tend to cost you at least one cooking pot, a blowpipe and a parang.

dialogue reprinted with permission of Eric Hansen [3]

Hardly head-hunters, these particular Borneo natives!
You know what? A "Census Bureau " in the rainforest is sheer monkey business! How can you possibly catalogue populations like ours which are undergoing traumatic shifts?! We are being killed off by disease and malnutrition. And spiritually, our younger members reject the traditional ways. Meanwhile, animals are dying off whom we have never seen!

Some degree of extinction is normal, in the course of evolution. Nature has her own "weeding process." But, due to extremely mismanaged human intervention in the tropical forests, we are losing species at well over 100 times the normal rate.
HI! I'm CHARLES DARWIN
There has not been such an epidemic of extinctions for 65 million years!
Within a quarter of a century, a quarter of the world's species may vanish! Now, there's a monstrous Census approximation! And while the precise effects of this "ecological holocaust" can not be predicted, it just don't look good for anyone interested in long-term survival...

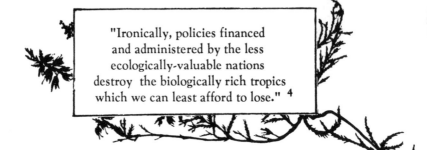

All creatures, including humankind, share their habitats'
peril. As 140,000 acres of tropical forest are destroyed
or degraded each day, anywhere from 50 to 150 varieties
of life become extinct. By the time you finish reading
this book, perhaps 3 or 4 of the Earth's species will have
perished— and we'll never know who they were.

Johnny, we hardly knew ye!

This blank page commemorates the human beings
and the animal, plant and microbe species already
annihilated in the "epoch of tropical deforestation."

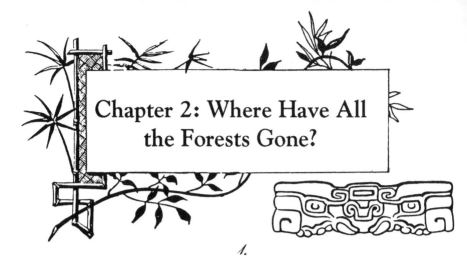

Chapter 2: Where Have All the Forests Gone?

1.

I lift my voice in wailing. I am afflicted,
as I remember that we must leave the
beautiful flowers, the noble songs; let us
enjoy ourselves for a while, let us sing,
for we must depart forever, we are to be
destroyed in our dwelling place.

2.

It is indeed known to our friends
how it pains and angers me that never
again can they be born, never again be
young on this earth.

3.

Yet a little while with them here,
then nevermore shall I be with them,
nevermore enjoy them, nevermore
know them.

4.

Where shall my soul dwell? Where
is my home? I am miserable on earth.

5.

We take, we unwind the jewels, the
blue flowers are woven over the yellow
ones, that we may give them to the
children.

6.

Let my soul be draped in various
flowers; let it be intoxicated by
them; for soon I must weeping go
before the face of our Mother.

— AZTEC LAMENT

"Takes more than guns to kill a man," said Chico, "I didn't die..."

HI! I'm CHICO MENDES

Since my murder by gunshot in December, 1988, I've been looking over this crazy world, and I can tell you : it's much easier on this side! Now I'm all over the place -- in books, films, even on a float in Rio's 1990 Carnivale! When I was acting among people it was always hard. It took years before anyone listened to what we rubber tappers in Brazil were saying! It took, at the very least, 45 blockades over a decade or more. Hundreds of families stood in lines to keep those bulldozers from coming. And they're still coming. I knew it wouldn't end. And the death threats don't end either. I may die many thousands of deaths to save more rainforest acres. Or I may vanish truly when no trees are left standing...

"What we demand," I remember saying a few months before the ranchers shot me, "is a complete re-orientation of Brazil's approach to the Amazon. It is the last hope for the rainforest, which is the last hope for humanity."

I am heartened by the appointment of Dr. Jose Lutzenberger as Secretary of the Environment. He has truly worked on behalf of Brazil's 68,500 rubber-tapper families.

But, folks, **this is some bloody business.** Ranchers, farmers and loggers are as passionate about their plans for the forest as we who fight to create extractive reserves, parks, and biospheres. I see loggers setting fire in Guatemala, I see Thai villagers arrested for defending their National Reserve Forest from a paper plantation, I see native Amazonians poisoned by mercury from mines, dying in pain from diseases to which they're not immune, I see fish drenched by oil spills further west, I see native women raped and prostituted, I see children stricken with diarrhea from water pollution while their parents barricade logging trucks in Malaysia, later to be tortured and imprisoned by the secret police... **and it's a hard rainforest, gonna fall!**

"White people have invented the word *environment*, but my people are part of the environment... the forest is like my mother and my father, it is they who have raised me.... In the forest exists the free spirit, the good spirit that is protecting the Earth..."

-- Davi Yanomami, [5]
Spokesman of the Yanomami

For three years we have been sick: our limbs numb, our vision weakening, 90% of us are infected with malaria. Mercury has poisoned our rivers and fish. The food chain is collapsing. We starve as our game die off or move away. My ancient people have never known such misery. Gold mining has resulted in genocide, ethnocide, murder of the Yanomami!

Brazil

The Brazilian government gives mixed messages: First they constitutionally protect the Yanomami territory. Then, President Sarney annuls his own legislation, and permits 45,000 gold miners to set up camp and dig mines. But next thing you know, in 1990 they're dynamiting our illegal landing strips and telling us, get lost! What's next?

If I strike gold I can buy land of my own. I won't need to sweat and labor day after filthy day!

What you gringo conservationists don't know is the real "law of the jungle." 100 years ago rubber tappers probably killed native tribes. When you gotta eat you gotta eat.

You who shout 'save the rainforests!'
Save every ooey gooey worm and ameba!
Would you care to EAT some of those?
We would have to, had we not wood with which to cook. Two billion of us, your fellow human beings in the Third World, are in desperate need of fuel wood. Are a bunch of sloths and ticks more important than our health and hunger?

Why are native tribes glorified as victims while we landless peasants and itinerant squatters are barely feeding our families? You think land is distributed fairly in Latin America? 7% of land owners here control 93% of arable lands. Meanwhile, the poorest third of us burn whatever forest we can find to raise crops on 1% of the land. It's like that in Africa and Asia as well. The elite of the 'developing world' don't cut us much slack!

You want to see rainforests?
Well, we want to see food stamps!
Subsidize us, and we'll quit
slash-and-burning!

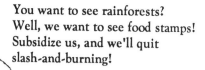

"It's more like slash

and trash."

Slash and burn farming is based on the false assumption
that soil which excellently sustains rainforests could
support ranching and agriculture. Yet such soil stripped
of its forest cover loses its nutrients and quickly becomes
sterile and useless. Peasants who attempt to farm on this land
find themselves continually moving on and leaving barren,
exhausted plots of land behind them.

Wish you gringo multilateral banks
would make up your minds! First
you offer us "development business
loans," encouraging us to scorch the
forests and create cattle pastures.
Next thing we know you're hollering
that our burning forests are emitting
too much carbon dioxide and cows are
a wasteful use of land, and Burger
King don't want our imports! I really
wonder about you guys...

What's Wrong With This Picture?

This harmless and stupid-looking beast is a prime cause of deforestation in Latin America.

Land required to feed cattle = 20 times land required to directly feed people.

Grazing herds stamp through the mud and push away rainwater and loose topsoil, further sterilizing their "pastures."

Rainforest soil is notoriously poor in nutrients. Unlike temperate zone pastures, which remain fertile for decades, rainforest soil stripped of its vegetation is exhausted within two or three crop seasons. The cattle who consume grain or , more often, grass from such land are lean and muscular, often used in cheap processed meats and pet food.

While tropical pastures last longer than croplands, few remain intact for more than a decade. Is one fast-food burger worth fifty-five square feet of rainforest, including one large tree and inestimable numbers of plants and animals?

Where's the beef?

Less than 10% of catttle raised on 30 million acres of Latin American ranches became beef.

Yo! *Where's the beef?*

The ranchers are too poor to eat their own beef.

Oklahoma, where the grass grows...

Wish I were there. This soil is a scam!

The First World subsidizes us to convert this most splendid, biologically powerful forest into barren prairies in the name of mystery meat and bullsh.....

37

Ecuador

Did I hear someone say 'propane?"
What a marvelous idea! Our buddies
in Ecuadorian government have promised
us half of Yasuni for industry. And we struck
oil in seven out of ten test wells, so--
we're game!

Didn't Arco, Texaco and Occidental
score in Ecuadorian forests several
miles away? Why shouldn't CONOCO?

But Conoco did not. In the autumn of 1991,
Conoco scrapped its Ecuador agenda. Public
pressure, exerted notably through the San Francisco-
based Rainforest Action Network, discouraged
a major corporation from mining the forest
and endangering its inhabitants.

"However, no sooner did CONOCO throw in the
towel than another oil company... Maxus, stepped
in as the lead developer of the block 16 oil site
in eastern Ecuador." --Randy Hayes.
RAINFOREST ACTION NETWORK

Oh well. Maybe we'll round up some
Fundamentalist missionaries. They do
such a good job pacifying restless natives!

We, the Huaorani people of Ecuador, have one message for Arco, Texaco, CONOCO and all the other CO-dependents enabling your society's addiction to fossil fuels: dry up!

Did you know that huge quantities of petroleum can be squeezed from palm oil and other foliage?

Would you tolerate tresspassers who use your home as a sewer and morgue?

Benzene, toluene, napthalene don't belong in our ground-water!

Your roads, which you say are "off limits to farmers, ranchers and loggers," will pave their way into our territory.

You send your missionaries to "civilize" us. They suggest we kill off our shamans and war with neighboring tribes. Convenient for you! You can keep your "civilization" with its atrocious oil spills, ethical foul play and spiritually bankrupt illusions. Legally, this land is ours, and we wish to live well.

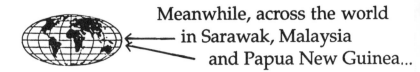

Meanwhile, across the world
in Sarawak, Malaysia
and Papua New Guinea...

Japan is the world's Number One importer of tropical hardwoods.

Our thinking is very pragmatic: these woods are both durable and beautiful, therefore profitable. Honshu Paper was the first company in the world to practice clear cutting, having obtained a concession in Papua New Guinea.

When timber runs out in the Philippines, Malaysia, and Southeast Asian peninsulas, Japan will do business in Papua New Guinea and Brazil! We must keep trees at home for watershed protection, and beauty.

Guess who is the Number 2 world importer of tropical timber?

We try harder!

Southeast Asia's forests include some of the most unusual tree species -- like the majestic dipterocarp. Scores of plants and animals are found only in Borneo. Yet these special forests disappear more quickly than any others in the world! **And only 10% of cleared virgin forest ends up in a finished product.** Is such virginity worth losing?

Timber barons... local governments... logging concessions, overseas corporations...

They *weave a wicked web!* Third World countries, desperate for foreign exchange, log at tenfold the rate that forests naturally regenerate. Southeast Asia may be ahead of the game now, but what happens in five to ten denuded years? Who will have anything? Not even we Malaysian silk spiders!

A.L. Clement

41

You processed-meat head!
You want to drill into a
volcano! This 'won't harm
the environment?!' Say what?!!

*Aloha! Here I am on Hawaii's Big Island.
True Geothermal Company of Wyoming
hopes to build a 500-megawatt
power plant or two. Geothermal drilling
does not harm the environment, and these
power projects could be the answer to
Hawaii's energy demands. But, wouldn't
you know it? A bunch of
greenies are supporting
restless natives again.
Recently, they staged
Hawaii's biggest public
demonstration in history!
And just listen to what
the primitives say: our drilling site,
located in the Wao Kele O Puna
rainforest, is a 'manifestation of
their sacred goddess!' What next, I ask you!*

*But they've managed to file an injunction against further funding
of our project. We gotta get an Environmental Impact Statement
ratified or we may lose some creditors. Good thing we have
a pal in office. As of Summer '91, Governor John Waihee hasn't
exactly put the padlock on our drills, EIS or not, "goddess" or not!*

Try breathing hydrogen sulfide if you're elderly, pregnant or ill. You might become extinct!

Interestingly, American freedom of worship does not apply to all religions. We Hawaiians pray each day to Pele, the volcano. That is one manifestation of her. She is also the lava, the steam, the heat force, the very ground. It is a violation of our worship to drill holes into her body, to harness her steam and destroy her rainforest for profit. But do you think the courts honor our faith?

They Call Us "Amazon North..."

Has anyone noticed a pattern in the pages you've just read?

Mercury consumed by Cree Indians downstream of La Grande hydroelectric complex is as noxious as mercury consumed by Yanomami near the illegal gold mines in Brazil.

Industry has no regard for Nature. Don't matter where it happens. The Amazon is everywhere these days!

The "Amazon" Model of Postwar Megaprojects

Hydro - QuEbec, Manitoba Hydro, + Ontario Hydro Company(ies), of *Canada*

under the financial auspices of *U.S. + European loans*

has bid for land in *Hudson Bay/James Bay Bioregion* to create *The Great Whale hydroelectric power developments*, regardless of

any damage this industry might bring to the local people, the land, animals or the world at large. *Beluga whales, caribou+ freshwater seals* have already

become extinct or endangered in the experimental phases of this project.

Laborers employed are underpaid, live in uncomfortable camps,

and often abuse the native population. *Mercury* pollutes

the water, *flooding* destroys the topsoil, and *(Not Applicable)*

fouls the air. Although the land in question legally belongs to its

indigenous people, *Cree and Inuit*, the government has

annuled or violated its own law, hoping to cash in on a piece of the action.

What can I say? It's progress! It's necessary! As for drowned caribou-- that was an act of God!

10,000 caribou drowned in 1984. Their bloated carcasses lined the banks of Quebec's Caniapicscau River in the aftermath of a hydroelectric flood.

"One wonders at the hubris of creatures that inflict so much damage on the Earth and then declare themselves its stewards or healers." --Lawrence E. Joseph, author of *Gaia: the Growth of an Idea* [6]

More than anything, war is a hideous, disgusting mess! Yuck! Look at those contorted corpses! Look at those totalled cities, fires, famines and dead forests! People wage war, all species of the earth pay.

They don't like bugs. How do they think we like defoliants and that eerie, harrowing "biological" warfare?

And <u>no one</u> gains! Have you noticed that lately, all wars seem to occur in resource-rich lands? Precisely those coveted resources-- oil, timber, metals-- are sacrificed to nothing other than a fashion show of state-of-the-art bombers! No heroic national legends can justify this tragic waste-- I'm sorry.

Wars bring about slash-and-burn farming. People flee big cities and have to survive in the forests. It happened in Panama in '89...

But nuclear explosion would render slash and burn farming a trivial injury, from which forests might eventually recover!

Well now wait. While ugly, wars do stimulate technological development and provide commercial enterprises with new markets.

47

Which of us do you mean?

No one individual or one corporation or one government is unique in wiping its toxic butt on a rainforest. It's the mentality of world-wide market economy! It's a particular value system...

... or lack of value system

Well, what about you, my pretty little reckless girl?

Don't you have a stove and refrigerator?

Don't you love a hot shower?

Don't you ride cars and liberally consume paper?

All of the above. But there's an important distinction to be made: I enjoy heat and transportation, not fossil fuels. I could envision a reasonably comfortable life which would not destroy the earth. I would vastly prefer that. I'd lose nothing! It's YOU who would lose, and that's why you run rampant with your windfall profit schemes: you know you will lose one day!

Who, me? I happen to be optimistic! I think positive, and I happen to know a multi-billion dollar industry when I see one. You're probably just jealous!

No way. If I were you, I couldn't face myself. You reek of death!

Hmm. Now why is it that in a rainforest, decomposers (who also "reek of death") are so valued that you advise we inconvenience ourselves to preserve them -- in history volcanos have erupted, land masses have shifted, comets have struck -- and that's all okay, but what I'm doing is not? Doesn't it ever occur to you sentimentalists that my actions are also natural? And-- may I point out -- in history, traumatic species losses sometimes were thought to trigger evolution! It's rather like clipping your trees and hedges so they grow! I may be doing the world a great service!

Well, maybe you are. At the rate you're going the human species is bound to become extinct. Maybe, once the planet recovers from our ravages, evolution will once again flourish!

51

Chapter 3: Life After Forests' Death?

" What you create today, how you say it, how you feel it, how you manifest it as you walk upon the earth, comes back to you. It always goes in a full circle. It always comes back. " —— Hemispheric Movement of Indigenous Peoples, 1977.

HI! I'm
SIR ISAAC
NEWTON

Let us not be fooled
By what we do not see.
When an apple falls --
Such is "Gravity!"
When rainforests fall,
Consequences prove grave.
The elements respond
As humankind behaves.

It's Natural Law.

EARTH

We are spirit men **Eradbatli** and **Kumail-Kumail** from the Northern Arnhem Land in Australia.

We roam ashen desert which had been rainforest. Miles and miles we look, and no trees protect the soil. Already parched and weakened by tropical sun, topsoil is flagellated by daily storms. Barren and brittle land no longer stirs with unseen creatures regenerating nutrients of decayed plants. Nothing can grow.

Upon this once most fertile land, nothing grows! Not rice, not export crops, not medicinal plants, not forests, not hopes. Not for scores of years, if ever again.

Instead, topsoil is washed
away by heavy rains into
rivers, or sent tumbling
down deforested slopes
by land slips and earthquakes.
Wasted, eroded, exhausted,
the land can no longer
feed or sustain anybody.

55

WATER

I am **Oshun**, Nigerian river goddess of Love. To the Yoruba people, I represent beauty, flirtation, the arts, pleasure, sensuality, color. I walk with the river's flow in my hips and belly, I bring sweet honey to the children, I ring a brass bell and say:

BAD HEAD, BECOME GOOD!

As rivers become silted up with eroded topsoil they no longer sing! They swell up and inundate croplands, villages, dams, and reservoirs. Then they withhold for months. All nearby water supplies, both urban and rural, are endangered. Our little scaled brothers who bring protein to the people are poisoned by mercury deposits. The river betrays all who would bathe and drink.

THINK SERIOUSLY! Although you may not see it happen before your eyes, rainforests preserve water supplies. Trees and plants recycle rain back into the skies. When you cut down tropical (or any) forests, you mess with rainfall and evapotranspiration cycles! In other words, **the more forests you cut, the more moisture you remove from the climate.**

Beware of possibilites associated with the 'greenhouse effect,' to which deforestation contributes: tidal rises, serious coastal flooding in years to come.

So what you are doing, and I'll be very precise so that even the thickest heads get it, is: **creating a world of erratic drought and flooding patterns, of hydro-electric dams rendered useless, of rivers lethally polluted, of less and less rainfall.** Look at the Panama Canal, for example. Nearby rainforests were burned down. Now, sedimentation and diminished rainfall have reduced water levels in the canal to the point of obstructing ship passage.

Water is a beautiful, tender, cleansing friend... and a violent enemy.

FIRE

I am **Pele**, Hawaiian
goddess of Everlasting Fire.
You wouldn't expect to find
me in a book about rainforests,
with all those wet, green, mossy,
misty connotations. But here I
am with good news, but more
bad news, alas.

The good news: our planet
is not static. Elements co-mingle.
For many years, fires have helped
forests to regenerate themselves,
and are often a natural part of the
forest's cycle. Fire has been a
tremendous gift to all peoples.

The bad news: fire is being
misunderstood, and abused in
the tropical forests. Too many flames
devour greenery which would
have photosynthesized all excess
carbon dioxide and then released oxygen.

The last thing Earth's atmosphere
needs is more carbon dioxide,
and over a billion tons are added each
year when tropical forests burn at
this menacing rate.

And can you imagine local fire storms
in Amazonia, mini-tornadoes, thunder,
lightening, skies gray and dense with
smoke?

And when flames subside and
skies clear, deforested land reflects
sunshine back into space. **Earth
becomes more shiny and suseptible
to solar radiation without the
forests' protective opacity.**

One need not be supernatural or immortal to realize that, in this time of dangerously accumulating 'greenhouse gases' in the atmosphere, we need tropical forests more than ever to counterbalance trends of global warming. While not exactly "lungs of Earth" -- for our own lungs inhale oxygen and exhale carbon dioxide -- the rainforests do stablize our climates worldwide, and maintain humidity, wind and convection patterns.

Have you noticed any weather changes in recent years? Beware: **As rainforests disappear, cyclones, hurricanes, heat waves and dry spells may hit where least expected.**

What exactly is 'The Greenhouse Effect'?

People who live in glass houses should not throw ozones!

Like greenhouse glass, earth's
atmosphere is designed to modify
the sun's rays. Ozone, a gas concentrated
in the stratosphere, protects life on
earth from ultraviolet radiation.
Radiation which reaches the earth
is photosynthesized by plants
or absorbed by land and water as heat.
Infrared heat then radiates back into space.
It is trapped by natural "greenhouse
gases" which delay its passage through
the atmosphere and keep the climate
warm enough to support life. However,
a surplus of greenhouse gases
such as carbon dioxide may prove to be
"overkill." Too much heat would remain.
**Global temperatures may rise enough,
in the next century, to severely disrupt
rainfall patterns and soil structures all
over the planet. This ominous probability,
with its range of unknown consequences,
is called "The Greenhouse Effect."**

We definitely know, however, that
reducing greenhouse gas emissions will
slow global warming, and that burning rainforests
accomplish the reverse. The rainforests also
provide protective cloud cover which serves to
cool temperatures.

*Bah, humbug! All these nasty,
depressing predictions. And
yet life goes on. I wake each day,
the sky is blue or cloudy, I have
coffee. I hear of cyclones in
India, greenhouse gases,
solar radiation, but life goes on!*

Some populations are more
immediately impacted by the loss of
rainforests than others. Those living
in forests naturally suffer first.
**But all lives and ecosystems are
jeopardized by long-term effects.** Forests
and their fossilized remains contain huge
deposits of inert, solid carbon.
When fossil fuels and forests are burned,
releasing massive quantities of carbon
dioxide, The Greenhouse Effect is
is quickened. Add this problem to those
of eroded soil, spoiled water, unnatural
"Natural Disasters" like floods and earthquakes brought on by deforestation, loss of
species, vegetation and cloud cover, the
advent of pests and diseases... and life on
Earth won't exactly resemble a picnic in Eden.

*I may not be an expert in karate,
but I do need my green belt for
protection!*

Once upon a time we revered them. Sacred groves were humanity's first temples. In some historical societies, he who felled a tree "died on the spot." All over the world, in different cultures, trees were believed to be magical and powerful, to incarnate deities or souls of the dead.

Ecologically as well as spiritually, trees stand between earth and heaven. They transform the sun's radiant energy into our raw materials of life. Through photosynthesis they circulate oxygen, through their cells and tissue they circulate water. They protect soil and generate food for all species. On hot summer days they shade us, in winter their wood burns in our fireplaces.

Despite their divinity, beauty and life-sustaining services, our species has progressed into brutalizers of trees.

Ever since the Iron Age equipped us with axes, they have been turned loose upon woodlands. In 13th Century Europe as in present-day Amazonia, forestry laws have been ignored and violated.

The rainforest crisis exemplifies our love-hate relationship with trees, since rainforests, the most dense and massive land vegetation, exemplify trees. Healing, photosynthesizing and moisture-circulating properties of all trees are optimal in the rainforests.
Destroying them will unravel life as we know it.

Conjure, if you will, the possibility of human life without trees. Over shadeless expanses of dust you would lug oxygen tanks, stopping now and then for a snack of flavored styrofoam.
All of your books and wooden furniture would be locked away from the poachers who conduct mad raids for fuelwood.
And as you do without paper and wood, so you do without fireplaces, fruit and blossoms.
Birds will die off, with nowhere to migrate when we fly south.
If this future appeals to you, don't bother turning the page.

Chapter 4: Protecting Our Rainforests

"*The forest makes no demands for its sustenance and extends generously the products of its life activity; it affords protection to all beings, offering shade even to the axeman who destroys it.*"

-- GAUTAMA BUDDHA

You've turned the page!
Thank you for agreeing that
a future without trees is not
worth corporate profits and
mass lifestyle "perks."
And now for the hard part.
Loving trees and glorying
in rainforest imagery are
easy to do. Working effectively
to conserve them takes time,
intelligence, care, cooperation,
will power and application.

Where do we begin
to bury the hatchet?

I'm wearing a
T-shirt and
being positive!

*How cute!
Get me one too.
I take an XL.
And I'd like a
boa constrictor
on it!*

SAVE
RAINFORESTS

Those of us who live in post-modern,
post-industrial states face inevitable
paradoxes: in the U.S., for example,
our tax and consumer dollars, as well
as our investment capital, sponsor
tropical deforestation. Who are we to
holler *STOP*? Who are we to exact
economic sacrifice of Third World
people who covet our highly
propagandized "standard of living,"
whose governments are overwhelmed
with foreign debt? And what kind of example
is our timber and fossil fuel management?
Don't we exploit our own rainforests in
Hawaii, Puerto Rico and the Virgin Islands?

Two points of departure may
inform our actions: 1. Improved
forestry policies at home will
impact the tropical nations,
and 2. Investment and consumer
dollars can be re-channeled to
support sustainable use of the
rainforests, and discourage
reckless and destructive business.

It's time to clean up our act at home!

Action Guidelines

1. WRITE LETTERS
When groups of consumers speak up,
big business and its cronies listen.

2. JOIN A RAINFOREST PROTECTION GROUP
There are plenty to choose from.
If none suits your approach, create one.

3. PUT YOUR MONEY WHERE YOUR MOUTH IS
Adopt rainforest land to be
held in trust and used by those who live there.
Support responsibly manufactured rainforest goods.

Did you know that
chewing gum often comes
from rainforest *chicle?*

Visit a rainforest or two on an 'eco-tour.'

4. READ MORE
You are no longer a "beginner." You now know
some rainforest "basics," but there is much more
to learn, and many books and journals to inform you.

5. WEAR A T-SHIRT AND THINK POSITIVE
Why not? Who says we can't have fun?
T-shirts often support organizations, and
they spread the word. Just don't stop there...

> *Havin' a wonderful time...*
> *wish you weren't here!*

If you believe that rainforest destruction imperils your life-support system, let your elected officials know. Tell agencies, banks and corporations -- the ABCs who fund deforestation abroad -- that you are informed and justifiably critical of their practices.

Point out that everyone's future and health is at stake when they mutilate tropical forests at the current rate. Point out that **many "development" endeavors in the rainforest defeat themselves --** such as the Perimetral Norte, a highway cut through Amazonia which was carelessly routed through flood areas. Remind them that in June 1991 a geothermal explosion in Hawaii poisoned the Puna rainforest and its community. Refer them to the hydroelectric dams which have been flooded into inutility, to the degraded watersheds, polluted rivers and coastal fisheries in the tropics. Quote how many tons of carbon dioxide are released into the atmosphere when forests are burned. **There are many unfortunate examples of foolishness.**

In light of this, convince legislators not to jettison or "fudge" environmental guidelines. Now is the time to develop and <u>enforce</u> them! Suggest to corporations that **economic appraisals of** rainforests consider **possible revenues from renewable, non-timber resources.** Sometimes these are more profitable than the messy "big tickets!" Demand that **environmental studies** and **consultation with local inhabitants** determine the destiny of any rainforest.

If this seems a lot of writing, and you're busy or tongue-tied, take some short-cuts. Share the labor with friends, assigning each an area of specialty. Buy a Gauguin or Henry Rousseau postcard and scrawl, "Havin' a wonderful time-- wish your wells/highways/mines **weren't** here!" Snip parts of this book into new collages. Or send a transvestite Strip-O-Gram. "When you denude forests, you never know what can happen!"

When they write back (as they will)...

Keep on their cases! Let them know you mean business. They want to pacify you, and hope that an initial blast of hot air will do the trick. Try to read not only between the lines, but between the words. What does "growth" mean, for example? Growth of what? Under what terms and at whose expense? Mind their words.

Remember, you do mean business -- their business. Collectively, all of our purchases and investments make or break them.

It's a bargaining chip!

Just as collectively, their policies and actions make or break all of our ecosystems!

Here are some worthy pen pals.
Initially, express your viewpoint
about rainforests and probe
them on their own, and on their
track records funding, legislating
or profiting from deforestation.
Be prepared. You may get enough hot
air in response to cause greenhouse gas
combustion in your mail box!

Government Officials:

President George Bush
The White House
1600 Pennsylvania Ave., NW
Washington, DC 20500

James Baker
Secretary of State
U.S. State Department
2201 C St.., NW
Washington, DC 20520

Secretary of Agriculture
U.S. Dept. of Agriculture
14th St. and Independence, S
Washington, DC 20250

Multinational and Development Banks and money funds:

President,
The World Bank
1818 H St., NW
Washington, DC 20433

Director,
International Money Fund
700 19th St., NW
Washington, DC

President, Inter-American
Development Bank
1808 17th St., NW
Washington, DC 20577

Administrator,
U.S. Agency for
International Development
320 21st St., NW
Washington, DC 20577

Regarding Hawaiian rainforests:

Governor John D. Waihee III
Executive Chamber
State Capitol,
Honolulu, Hawaii 96813

Senator Daniel Inouye
722 Hart Office Building
Washington, DC 02510

H.A. True, President
True Geothermal Company
PO Box 2360
Casper, WY 82602

Concerning international "free-trade" agreements, which would jeopardize environmental security:

Arthur Dunkel,
Director General
General Agreement on Tariff and Trade
54 Rue de Lausanne
1211 Geneva 21
SWITZERLAND

Secretary General,
United Nations,
New York, NY 10017

If banks lend the money and governments nod, corporations actually do the dirty work. At whatever remote, timeless, obscure location, you can bet someone's rigging up a well, cutting trees and poisoning local people. There are too many corporations to list here, and as many as possible should be contacted. Here are three rainforest "biggies":

D. W. Chamberlain, PhD
Senior Consultant, Environmental Sciences
ARCO International Oil and Gas
515 South Flower Street, Box 2679 T A
Los Angeles, CA 90051

Mr. Makihara, President and CEO
Mitsubishi International
520 Madison Avenue
New York, NY 10022

Constantine S. Nicandros, CEO
Conoco Inc.
600 N. Dairy Ashford Road
Houston, TX 77079

Thank them for leaving Ecuador. And keep'em out!

WRITE LETTERS!

(P.S. They regard each letter they receive as the equivalent of 500, in terms of public opinion.)

If you feel overwhelmed by
the complexity of this problem,
still uncertain about whom to
write and what to say, sick of the
litanies of noxious chemical compounds
which daily assault our environment,
if you're tired of hearing statistics
about how many acres of rainforest
are destroyed each year, day and second
and how innocent people are poisoned...
you're not alone.

Many people are angry and concerned
about the cruel fate of rainforests.
Hearteningly, rainforest protection
groups have banded together in the U.S.,
in Western Europe, Japan and Australia,
as well as in the tropical countries. This
represents an exciting possibility of working
in friendship, across cultural and geographic
boundries, to achieve commonly desired ends.

BUT--Is it even possible for
Americans to espouse
any cause without
dividing into factions?

No.

Of course viewpoints and strategies will vary from group to group. But it is important to bear in mind that everyone wants more or less the same outcome, and that the opposition is formidable. Learn which rainforest group most represents your own approach, send a yearly pittance, and you will already make a difference. In addition, you'll receive regularly updated reports on what is occuring in the endangered places and how your own words and consumer patterns may shape policy.

Bah, humbug! These groups do nothing! They don't change anything. They just take your money!

Oh bah humbug yourself! Groups have revolutionized public awareness of this crisis. How many books about rainforests existed 5 years ago?

Now we are deluged not only with books, but with magazine articles, TV specials, even interactive computer games about rainforest themes. But also, groups have purchased and protected land cooperatively with rainforest dwellers, organized product boycotts, identified corporations which damage the forest, and funded ethical research and business projects.

A nine-year-old kid in Sweden started a group called Children's Rainforest which has transformed $600,000.00 of Central American debt into funds which are protecting a Costa Rican rainforest.

"Never doubt that a small group of thoughtful, committed citizens can change the world; indeed, it's the only thing that ever has."

--anthropologist Margaret Mead

"Two or three people gathered together in the name of truth, beauty, overmind consciousness, could... direct lightening flashes of electric power to slash across and destroy the world of dead, murky thought,... could bring the whole force of this power back into the world."

--poet "HD" [7]

"People ask me how I became involved (in protecting the Puna rainforest), I tell them, I was born involved.'
　　--poet W.S. Merwin [8]

"Of course, our power to shape reality has limits. Reality also has the power to shape us... Within (given) sets of circumstances we can make choices that will shape our future. But reality is a collective event and can be changed only by collective action."
　　--writer and activist Starhawk [9]

"If everyone stopped analyzing for ten minutes and did something instead, you'd see a difference in the world."
　　--Nancy Macdonald, founder
　　Spanish Refugee Aid Society [10]

Now that you're convinced it's worthwhile to join a rainforest group, here is a list of several. These coalitions focus exclusively on rainforest issues:

Children's Rainforest
PO Box 936
Lewiston, ME 04240
(207) 784-1069

Rainforest Action Network
301 Broadway, Suite A
San Francisco, CA 94133
(415) 398-4404

Earth First!
Tropical Timber Project
PO Box 83
Canyon, NY 13617

Rainforest Alliance
270 Lafayette Street, Suite 512
New York, NY 10012
(212) 941-1900

Pele Defense Fund
PO Box 404
Volcano, HI 96875

Amanaka'a
494 Broadway
New York, NY 10012

Groups which work with indigenous rainforest peoples to secure their rights to decide their own futures:

Coordinating Body for Indigenous People's Organization for the Amazon Basin
1101 Orleans St.
New Orleans, LA 70116

Cultural Survival
11 Divinity Ave.
Cambridge, MA 02138
(617) 495-2562

Survival International
310 Edgware Road
London W2 1DY
ENGLAND

Other conservation groups include
some rainforest programs within
a broader base of environmental
activism:

Environmental Defense Fund
1616 P St., NW
Washington, DC 20036
(202) 387-3500

Friends of the Earth
218 D Street, SE
Washington, DC 20003
(202) 544-2600

Global Tomorrow Coalition
1325 G St., NW, Suite 915
Washington, DC 20005
(202) 628-4016

Greenpeace
1436 U Street, NW
Washington, DC 20009
(202) 462-1177

National Resources Defense Council
1350 New York Ave., NW
Washington, DC 20005
(202) 783-7800

Sierra Club
730 Polk Street
San Francisco, CA 94009
(415) 776-2211

Union of Concerned Scientists
26 Church Street
Cambridge, MA 02238

The Grateful Dead did it -- guess I can too!

ADOPT RAINFOREST LAND

Now that adopting inanimate "Cabbage Patch Kids" is passé, we may wish to adopt some highly alive tracts of land, namely, acres of rainforest. Various environmental groups offer inexpensive or 'pay-what-you-want' land adoption programs. But we must support those groups who establish cooperative contact with the local people. After all, rainforests are their home, and enough outsiders have already meddled with it. We would not wish to further this unfortunate trend. Rather, by working with forest inhabitants, we might fruitfully exchange information and put the power of ownership back into their own hands.

FUNDACAO BIODIVERSITAS
(Biodiversitas Foundation)
Rua Bueno Brandao, 372
Santa Tereza-31010
Belo Horizonte/ MG Brazil

one option

For information on land adoption:
Biodiversitas Foundation,
Tropical Forest Fund
Ms. Heloisa Barreto Edwards
Development Advisor to the President
PO Box 60223
Palo Alto, CA 94306

Is this what is meant by a debt-for-Nature swap?

The Biodiversitas Foundation acknowledges that **Naomi Rosenblatt** has generously donated toward the purchase of **Two** acre(s) of Brazilian Tropical Rainforest land to be preserved and held in perpetuity in its natural state as a trust for the peoples of the Earth.

PRESIDENT-BOARD OF DIRECTORS

DEVELOPMENT ADVISOR

No. That's when special groups buy a country's foreign debt at a discount, then sell it back to that country's banks. Then it can be invested in conservation and sustainable use.

SAVE
RAINFORESTS

SUSTAINABLE USE

What does **"sustainable use"** mean?

It means keeping the rainforests around for a rainy day... it means cultivating renewable resources rather than trashing it all for a one-shot deal... it means **method, not madness!**

No one knows more about their local ecosystems than those who have lived there over millennia. Generations have learned how to maximize the benefits of plants, herbs, barks, fruits, animals and subsistence crops. A wealth of orally transmitted knowledge dies when such aboriginal cultures die.

We no longer know what's "natural," and what's "cultivated."

What we define as "sustainable use" of forest resources has long and skillfully been practiced by rainforest dwellers worldwide. In the simple, natural act of creating 'backyard gardens,' native peoples have not only preserved, but enhanced the biological diversity around them. We may still be reaping benefits of forest management practiced hundreds of years earlier. For example, it has been thought that the densities of economically valuable trees, such as the chicle or Brazil nut trees found in Central America, or the durian trees in Malaysia, reflect their conscious cultivation centuries ago. It is also possible that absences of such seedlings signify soil exhaustion and over-harvesting, typical of imposed "monocultural" models.

Indigenous forest peoples and industrialized peoples could help each other tremendously now. Modern record-keeping systems might organize and expand upon native peoples' knowledge, and time-tested experience.

ETHNO-BOTANY

Ethno-botany = Anthropology + Botany

Tropical deforestation makes me sick!!

"Tropical forests represent nature's main storehouse of raw materials for modern medicine."

--Dr. Norman Myers [13]

Even butterflies contain anti-cancer compounds!

Less than 1 in 100 tropical plants are thoroughly studied for medicinal potentials. Yet, the slim percentage of flora already analyzed has yielded cures or possible therapies for such diseases as: migraines, cystic fibrosis, multiple sclerosis, cancer, leukemia, cholera, malaria, dysentery, ulcers, syphillis, hypertension,... even AIDS.

Rainforest - derived compounds are present in disinfectants, birth control pills, aspirins, sedatives, antibiotics, purgatives, local anesthetics and more.

God has made a cure for every disease out there.

Maybe so, but we can't find it if we're throwing it away.

The rainforests contain more alkaloid, antibacterial concentrates than anywhere else on earth.

That's right. 25% of our pharmaceutical drugs come from the 1% of intensively screened and studied rainforest flora.

You'd think the remaining 99% might offer something of interest, wouldn't you?

Well, that's why I'm here. There is still some forest left which has not been converted to chopsticks, toothpicks, cardboard or dog food.

Dr. Michael J. Balick (pictured above) is Director of The New York Botanical Garden's Institute of Economic Botany. Since 1987 Dr. Balick has spent 2-3 months a year in Belize studying with local medicine people. Some of his work has been funded by the U.S. government and a contact from the National Cancer Institute.

83

"The world's richest ecosystems also support millions of the world's poorest people; only by linking forest protection to development for the poor will either goal materialize."
—researcher John C. Ryan, [11] Worldwatch Institute

"Nobody believes the rainforests will be saved just because they are beautiful or.. essential to the long-term health of the planet... or because they are home to endangered groups... the hope is that sustainable products will become so valuable they will offer some measure of protection for the rainforests." [12]

Sorry, pal -- nothing will sustain me like timber!

You're cutting off your nose to spite your face! Renewable non-timber resources often yield higher net revenues than those based on conversion!

Wow! Check out this list! Maybe I really have been barking up the wrong tree -- or cutting down the wrong forests!

LIST OF NON -TIMBER RAINFOREST PRODUCTS:

FRUITS
NUTS
WAXES
PIGMENTS
DYES
SWEETENERS
HONEY
COFFEE
VITAMINS
MEDICINES
ESSENTIAL OILS
EDIBLE OILS
BALMS

RATTAN
LATEX (RUBBER)
GUMS
RESINS
CHICLE
VANILLA
TERPENS
PECTINS
EXUDATES
ELASTICS
PLANT-GENERATED
  FUELS AND PETROLEUM
ETC.

"Romantic notions about the rainforest should not become prisons for those who inhabit it. From their point of view, it's use it or lose it."

-- Jason Clay, [14]
Research Director,
Cultural Survival

ECO-TOURISM

Tropical botanists are not the only travelers to visit rainforests "sustainably." Anyone can be an "eco-tourist."

Eco-tourism offers journeys to endangered places which, in turn, protect them.
At best, this alternative tourist industry provides local people with a financial alternative to land destruction. Here is yet another way to prove that live forests can generate as much, if not more, income than dead ones.

But when you visit, be a good guest!

Ecotour Expeditions
POB 1066
Cambridge, MA 02238-1066

International Expeditions
1 Environs Park,
Helena, Alaska 35080

Geo Expeditions
POB 3656
Sonora, CA 95370

The Ecotourism Society
POB 755
N. Bennington, VT 05257

Willimetz Tours
HC 68
Box 113
Cushing, Maine 04563
(207) 354-8966

Here's a bold "Invitation au Voyage." These small foundations conduct retreats in cooperation with local shamans and medicine people. Such encounters can prove memorable.

The Dance of the Deer Foundation
Center for Shamanic Studies
POB 699
Soquel, CA 95073

The Ojai Foundation
POB 1620
Ojai, CA 93024

The New York Open Center
83 Spring St
New York, NY 10012

The Upaya Foundation
POB 359
Crestone, CO 81131-0359

What's the scoop at Ben and Jerry's?

Oh -- you mean Rainforest Crunch flavored ice cream!

Here's the story. Decide for yourself what you think: Once upon a time, a nice Jewish boy from Vermont named Ben went to a Grateful Dead Benefit for the rainforests in 1988. He wanted to literally put in his two cents for the cause, so he approached Jason Clay of Cultural Survival in Cambridge. Now this guy Clay is super-devoted. He would like to see sustainably cultivated products replace all existing ones on the market -- and not at some outrageous mark up. You know, inexpensive, for joes like us. And he's gone to rainforests, especially to Brazil, and started a Brazil nut cooperative and processing plant with natives and rubber tappers. **Rainforest Crunch** is a Brazil nut and cashew candy brittle sold on the retail market. A portion of all profits is channeled back to the forest people and their extractive reserve. So, Jason Clay told Ben to put some of this stuff in his famous Ben & Jerry's ice cream. And Ben did it. And now Ben and Jerry can hardly produce enough **Rainforest Crunch ice cream** to satisfy the demand!

"We don't have to sacrifice human rights or rape the environment to have development."
-- David Maybury-Lewis, founder of Cultural Survival [15]

These operations, located in the United States, manufacture foods, snacks and cosmetics using rainforest raw-materials. Many of them return a percentage of their profit to rainforest tribes, or to conservation groups.

Ben & Jerry's
Community Products, Inc.
RD 2, Box 1950
Montpelier, VT 05602
(802) 229-1840

Moonshine Trading Co.
P.O. Box 896
Winters, CA 95694
(916) 753-0601

New England Natural Bakers
107 Long Plain Rd., RDF #1
South Deerfield, MA 01373
(413) 665-8599

Tropical Botanicals
P.O. Box 1354
Rancho Santa Fe, CA 92067
Tollfree: (800) 777-1248

From the Rainforest
270 Lafayette Street, Suite 100
New York, Ny 10012
Tollfree: (800) 327-8496

Pueblo to People
P. O. Box 2545
Houston, TX 77252
Tollfree: (800) 843-5257

Blue Planet Trading Co.
717 Simundson Drive, #111
Point Roberts, WA 98281
(604) 251-4277

> I still need wood in my life -- but I'm trying to cut loose of irresponsibly manufactured timber. Here are some decent alternatives:

Edensaw Woods Ltd.
211 Seton Rd.
Port Townsend, WA 98368
(206) 385-7878

Gilmer Wood Co.
2211 NW Saint Helens Rd.
Portland, OR 97210
(503) 274-1271

Handloggers Hardwood
135 E. Francis Drake Blvd.
Larkspur, CA 94939
(415) 461-1180

The Luthier's Mercantile
412 Moore Lane
Healdsburg, CA 95448
(707) 433-1823

Mount Storm
7890 Bell Rd.
Windsor, CA 95492
(707) 838-3177

Pittsford Lumber Company
50 State Street
Pittsford, NY 14534
(716) 381-3489

Woodworkers Supply
5402 South 40th St.
Phoenix, AZ 85040
(602) 437-4415

Wild Iris Forestry
P.O. Box 1423
Redway, CA 95560
(707) 923-2344

89

EXTRACTIVE RESERVES

Extractive Reserves are protected areas of land from which local workers can harvest endemic produce. While they tend to be owned by the state, extractive reserves are locally managed. Therefore, they are said to represent more equitable models of land distribution than those in which wealthy land owners monopolize resource-rich areas and landless workers are "relocated" to the forests, fending for themselves via slash and burn farming with all its dead ends and wastefulness.

SAVE RAINFORESTS

Well, I'm sold! Tropical botanists are scouring the forest floor... farmers and rubber tappers are managing their own extractive reserves...

consumers and travelers are enjoying tropical elixirs... we have our rainforests and our market benefits. What's the problem? Why all the debate?

Just don't leap to conclusions!

There are clouds in every sky. For example, how do you know we can deliver non-timber goods at the rate, bulk and consistency that industry wants them.? Nature is not cost-effective in your terms.

And who would get a "property right" for anything created by the Great Spirit?

And what labor! In the past, we were enslaved on export crop plantations! For all its romance, the rubber boom was miserable for the tappers who worked long hours and made next to nothing. Even now the rubber tappers union in Brazil is threatened by competition from such large-scale plantations!

And who says the forest dwellers will remain ecological "noble savages?" Market pressures have been known to convert the best of us!

This is not a casual moment in natural or social history.

Rainforests supported human life as it evolved. Now human life is killing those very forests. Human life alone can rescue the rainforests from its own folly. It's up to each one of us alive.

The stakes are hundreds of feet high.

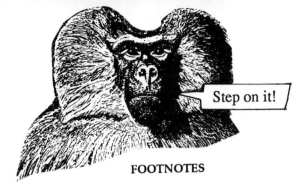

Step on it!

FOOTNOTES

1. Sir James George Frazer, *The Golden Bough*,
(New York: Macmillan Publishing Co., 1963), 126.

2. Diane Ackerman, "A Reporter at Large: Golden Monkies,"
The New Yorker, (June 24, 1991), 36.

3. Quotes paraphrased from Eric Hansen,
Stranger in the Forest:On Foot Across Borneo,
(Boston: Houghton Mifflin Co., 1988), and
from an author's interview with Mr. Hansen in May, 1991.

4. Quote paraphrased from Lawrence E. Joseph,
Gaia: the Growth of an Idea, (New York: St. Martin's Press,
1990), 81.

5. Davi Yanomami was quoted by Curtis Rist in
"Defenders of Rainforests," *Discovery*, (May 21, 1991).

6. Lawrence E. Joseph, See Reference Above, 195.

7. H.D., *Notes on Thought and Vision*, (San Francisco:
City Lights Books, 1982), 27.

8. W.S. Merwin stated this in a symposium connected
with the exhibition "Tropical Rainforests: A Disappearing
Treasure," on April 17, 1991, at the American Museum of
Natural History in New York City.

9. Starhawk, *Truth or Dare*, (San Francisco: Harper & Row,
1987), 24.

10. Nancy Macdonald said this in 1976 at a private dinner.

11. John C. Ryan, "Goods from the Woods," *Worldwatch
Magazine* , (August 1991).

12. Michael McCabe, "Marketing the Rainforests,"
San Francisco Chronicle, (October 1, 1989).

13. Norman Myers, *The Primary Source*, (New York and
London: WW Norton and Co., 1984), 210.

14. Jason Clay was quoted by Orna Feldman, *Harvard Magazine*,
Vol. 93, No.1.

15. David Maybury was quoted by Amy Miller, "Group Promotes
Ice Cream and Candy for Culture's Sake," *Cambridge Chronicle*,
(January 13, 1991).

GLOSSARY

Biomass: Trees, plants, other vegetation. This term may include animals living amidst the greenery.

Biological Diversity or **Biodiversity**: Range of different life forms and their gene pools.

Biosphere: Living portions of the earth. A **Biosphere Reserve** is a protected area which includes an inner zone that people may not harvest.

Carbon Dioxide (CO2): An incombustible gas made of carbon and oxygen.

Cloud Forest: A tropical forest located on a mountain, surrounded by heavy mists.

Convection Patterns: Atmospheric circulation of air masses with different temperatures.

Deciduous Forest: Forests which periodically shed leaves.

Decomposers: Tiny creatures who specialize in breaking organic matter into its separate parts.

Deforestation: Long-term or permanent removal of forests. Conversion of forests into croplands or mines.

Ecology: Branch of science which studies how living creatures and their environments interact.

Ecosystem: A biologically inter-dependent region which may be small as a pond or large as a planet.

Evergreen Forest: A forest in which leaves are not shed.

Geothermal: Pertaining to the earth's internal heat.

Indigenous: Original and native to a certain place.

Jungle: No, a rainforest is not a jungle. A jungle is a dense, tropical thicket, and corresponds to a rainforest's undergrowth or understory.

Microbe or **micro-organism**: Tiny creatures, germs, bacteria of microscopic size or smaller, protozoa.

Ozone: A type of oxygen, located in the stratosphere.

Parasite: An animal, plant or microbe who lives at another organism's expense without giving in return.

Photosynthesis: Complex process by which green plants feed themselves by transforming sunlight, water and carbon dioxide.

Savanna: Tropical desert or grassland.

Sedimentation: Build-up of matter, such as mud or silt in water.

Soil Erosion: Affliction and wearing away of soil by sun, wind or rain.

Solar: Pertaining to the sun. **Solar Radiation** is another word for sun rays.

Species: A type of plant or animal. Species group within the broader category of **genus**, as **breed** or **race** fall within a species.

Reading List

On the Rainforests and Tropical Deforestation:

Catherine Caufield, *In the Rainforest: Reports from a Strange, Beautiful, Imperiled World* (Chicago University Press, Chicago, 1984)

Adrian Forsyth & Ken Miyata, *Tropical Nature* (Charles Scribner & Sons, New York, 1984)

Suzanne Head & Robert Heinzman, *Lessons of the Rainforest* (Sierrra Club Books, San Francisco, 1990)

Joe Kane, *Running the Amazon* (Alfred A. Knopf, New York, 1989)

Scott Lewis, *The Rainforest Book* (Living Planet Press, Los Angeles, 1990)

Marius Jacobs, *The Tropical Rain Forest: A First Encounter* (Springer-Verlag, New York, 1988)

Kenton Miller & Laura Tangley, *Trees of Life: Saving Tropical Forests and Their Biological Wealth* (Beacon Press, Boston, 1991)

Norman Myers, *The Primary Source: Tropical Forests and Our Future* (W. W. Norton & Co., New York, 1984)

E.F. Moran, *Developing the Amazon* (Indiana University Press, Bloomington, 1981)

Donald Perry, *Life Above the Jungle Floor* (Simon & Schuster, New York, 1986)

Julie Sloan Denslow & Christine Padoch, *People of the Tropical Rainforest* (University of California Press, 1989)

Eric Hansen, *Stranger in the Forest: On Foot Across Borneo* (Houghton Mifflin, Boston, 1988)

Evelyne Hong, *Natives of Sarawak: Survival in Borneo's Vanishing Forests* (Institut Masyarakat, Malaysia, 1987)

Colin Turnbull, *The Forest People* (Simon & Schuster, New York, 1961)

On Global Ecology and Gaia Theory:

Lawrence E. Joseph, *Gaia: The Growth of an Idea* (St. Martin's Press, 1990)

James Lovelock, *The Ages of Gaia: A Biography of Our Living Earth* (W.W. Norton, New York, 1988)

Norman Myers, *The Gaia Atlas of Future Worlds* (Anchor Books, Doubleday, New York, 1990)

The Global Tomorrow Coalition, *The Global Ecology Handbook* (Beacon Press, Boston, 1990)